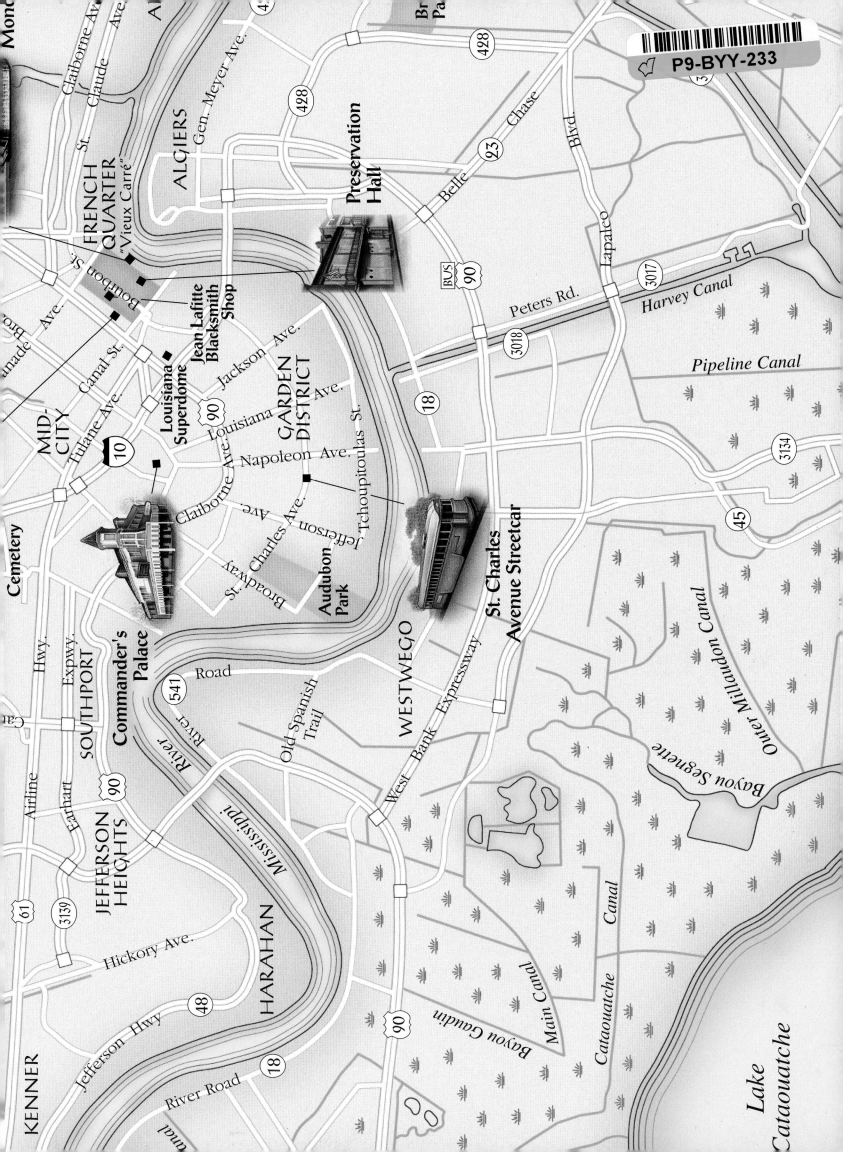

KENNER

Monc

FRENCH QUARTER "Vieux Carré"

ALGIERS

Claiborne Ave.
Claude
Ave.

Gen. Meyer Ave.

Bourbon St.

Preservation Hall

428

428

23

Chase

Belle

Blvd.

Lapalco

3017

BUS 90

Peters Rd.

Harvey Canal

3018

Pipeline Canal

Jean Lafitte Blacksmith Shop

Jackson Ave.

Canal St.

Louisiana Superdome

90

Ave.

GARDEN DISTRICT

18

3134

MID-CITY

Tulane Ave.

10

Louisiana

Napoleon Ave.

Tchoupitoulas St.

Jefferson Ave.

Claiborne Ave.

Charles Ave.

Cemetery

Broadway St.

Audubon Park

St. Charles Avenue Streetcar

45

Commander's Palace

Hwy.

Expwy.

SOUTHPORT

Road

Old Spanish Trail

WESTWEGO

West Bank Expressway

Outer Millaudon Canal

Bayou Segnette

541

River Road

Airline

Earhart

JEFFERSON HEIGHTS

90

61

3139

Jefferson Hwy

Hickory Ave.

HARAHAN

48

Mississippi

River

18

90

Main Canal

Cataouatche Canal

Bayou Gaudin

River Road

Lake Cataouatche

CAROL M. HIGHSMITH AND TED LANDPHAIR

NEW ORLEANS

A PHOTOGRAPHIC TOUR

CRESCENT BOOKS

NEW YORK

PAGE 1: Riverboats like the Natchez *played a crucial role in the commerce of the Mississippi River Valley, carrying cotton, sugar, rice—as well as New Orleans minstrels and gamblers—north-ward into the heart-land, and returning with lumber and grain. The* Natchez *is now strictly a pleasure boat, announcing its close-in tours of the river with jaunty tunes on its calliope. Long-distance cruises out of New Orleans aboard riverboats like the* Delta Queen *range as far as Pittsburgh as well. PAGES 2–3: A modern skyline would have been impossible had engineers not fig-ured a way to sink pilings deep into the city's soupy soil.*

Photographs copyright © 1997 by Carol M. Highsmith Text copyright © 1997 by Random House Value Publishing, Inc. All rights reserved under International and Pan-American Copyright Conventions.

No part of this book may be reproduced or transmitted in any form or by any means electronic or mechanical including photocopying, recording, or by any information storage and retrieval system, without permission in writing from the publisher.

This 1997 edition is published by Crescent Books®, an imprint of Random House Value Publishing, Inc., 201 East 50th Street, New York, N.Y. 10022.

Crescent Books® and design are registered trade-marks of Random House Value Publishing, Inc.

Random House New York • Toronto • London • Sydney • Auckland http://www.randomhouse.com/

Printed and bound in China

Library of Congress Cataloging-in-Publication Data
Highsmith, Carol M., 1946–
New Orleans / Carol M. Highsmith and Ted Landphair.
p. cm. — (A photographic tour)
ISBN 0-517-18610-1 (hc: alk. paper)
1. New Orleans (La.)—Tours.
2. New Orleans (La.)—Pictorial works.
I. Landphair, Ted, 1942–   . II. Title. III. Series:
Highsmith, Carol M., 1946–   Photographic tour.
F379.N53H54 1997   96–29726
917.63´3504´63—dc21   CIP

8 7 6 5 4

Project Editor: Donna Lee Lurker
Designed by Robert L. Wiser, Archetype Press, Inc., Washington, D.C.

All photographs by Carol M. Highsmith unless otherwise credited: map by XNR Productions, page 5; painting by John Michalopoulos, page 6; Library of Congress, pages 8–15, 18, 19; Café Du Monde, page 16; Antoine's Restaurant, pages 17, 20, 21

THE AUTHORS GRATEFULLY ACKNOWLEDGE THE SERVICES, ACCOMMODATIONS, AND SUPPORT PROVIDED BY

HILTON HOTELS CORPORATION

AND

THE NEW ORLEANS RIVERSIDE HILTON AND TOWERS

IN CONNECTION WITH THE COMPLETION OF THIS BOOK.

THE AUTHORS ALSO WISH TO THANK THE FOLLOWING FOR THEIR GENEROUS ASSISTANCE AND HOSPITALITY DURING THEIR VISITS TO NEW ORLEANS:

Errol Laborde, Editor, New Orleans Magazine

Gardner Kole

Ron Phillips and Sonja Remkes

Bonnie Warren Public Relations

Kit Wohl Public Relations

Blythewood Plantation, Amite Ipha Blache, Innkeeper

Andrew Jaeger's House of Seafood Julie Ott, Director of Public Relations

Assunta's Restaurant, Slidell Assunta Vitegliana Young, Chef

Commander's Palace Lally Brennan, Director of Public Relations

Palace Café Ti Martin, Proprietor

New Orleans Metropolitan Convention and Visitors Bureau, Inc. Christine DeCuir, Media Relations

Nicole and David Dickson

Juliette Landphair

American-Italian Renaissance Foundation Joseph Maselli, Founder

Morgan Lehr, Chief Engineer, Amoco Building

Tulane University Tom Grady, Public Relations

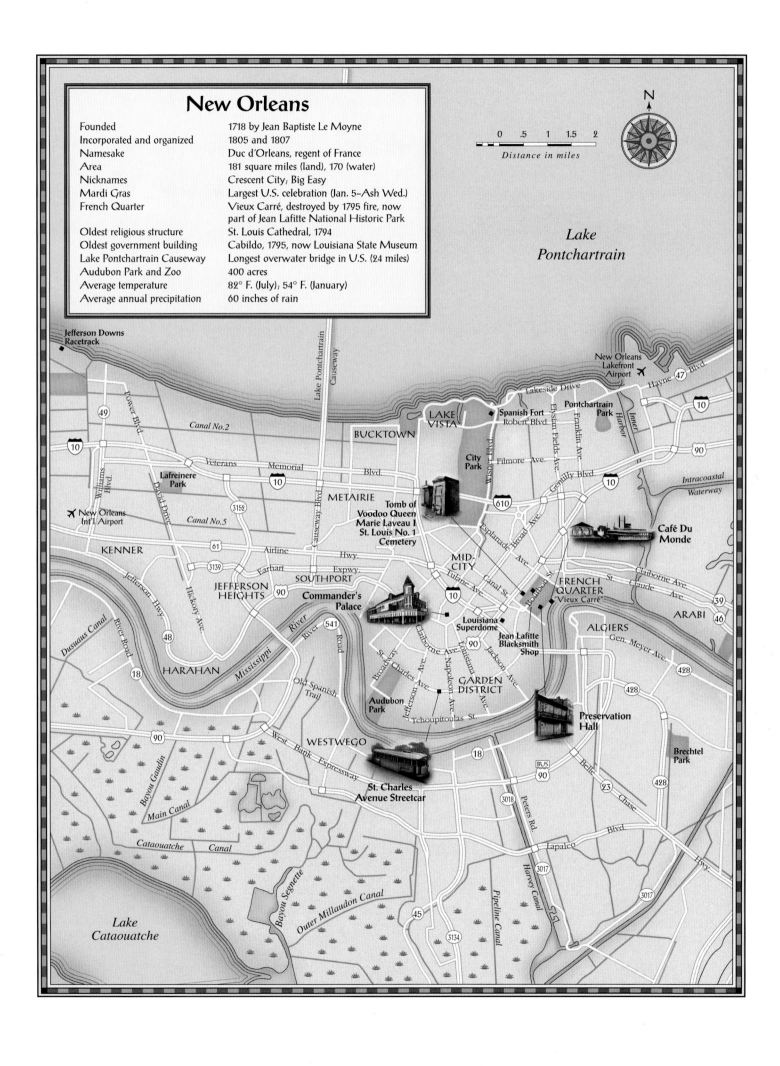

New Orleans

Founded	1718 by Jean Baptiste Le Moyne
Incorporated and organized	1805 and 1807
Namesake	Duc d'Orleans, regent of France
Area	181 square miles (land), 170 (water)
Nicknames	Crescent City; Big Easy
Mardi Gras	Largest U.S. celebration (Jan. 5–Ash Wed.)
French Quarter	Vieux Carré, destroyed by 1795 fire, now part of Jean Lafitte National Historic Park
Oldest religious structure	St. Louis Cathedral, 1794
Oldest government building	Cabildo, 1795, now Louisiana State Museum
Lake Pontchartrain Causeway	Longest overwater bridge in U.S. (24 miles)
Audubon Park and Zoo	400 acres
Average temperature	82° F. (July); 54° F. (January)
Average annual precipitation	60 inches of rain

N

0 .5 1 1.5 2
Distance in miles

Lake Pontchartrain

Jefferson Downs Racetrack

New Orleans Lakefront Airport

Hayne Blvd.

47

10

49

Power Blvd.

Canal No.2

BUCKTOWN

LAKE VISTA

Spanish Fort
Robert Blvd.

Pontchartrain Park

Lakeside Drive

Elysian Fields Ave.

Franklin Ave.

Inner Harbor

90

10

Williams Blvd.

Veterans
Memorial
Blvd.

10

City Park

West End Blvd.

Filmore Ave.

Gentilly Blvd.

10

Intracoastal Waterway

Lafreinere Park

David Drive

Canal No.5

3152

METAIRIE

Causeway Blvd.

Tomb of Voodoo Queen Marie Laveau I St. Louis No. 1 Cemetery

610

Esplanade Broad Ave.

Café Du Monde

New Orleans Int'l Airport

61

Airline Hwy.

MID-CITY

Canal St.

Claiborne Ave.

St. Claude Ave.

KENNER

3139

Earhart

SOUTHPORT

Expwy.

Tulane Ave.

10

FRENCH QUARTER "Vieux Carré"

39

Hickory Ave.

JEFFERSON HEIGHTS

90

Commander's Palace

541

Mississippi River

River Road

Louisiana Superdome

10

Jean Lafitte Blacksmith Shop

ARABI

46

ALGIERS

Gen. Meyer Ave.

Jefferson Hwy.

48

18

HARAHAN

Dusuaus Canal

River Road

Old Spanish Trail

Broadway

St. Charles Ave.

Claiborne Ave.

Napoleon Ave.

Louisiana Ave.

Jackson Ave.

GARDEN DISTRICT

90

428

428

Audubon Park

Jefferson Ave.

Tchoupitoulas St.

Preservation Hall

428

18

BUS 90

Belle Chase

Brechtel Park

90

West Bank Expressway

WESTWEGO

St. Charles Avenue Streetcar

3018

Peters Rd.

23

Bayou Gaudin

Main Canal

Cataouatche Canal

Harvey Canal

3017

Lapalco Blvd.

Hwy.

3017

Lake Cataouatche

Bayou Segnette

Outer Millaudon Canal

Pipeline Canal

45

3134

T HE HISTORIC SIGHTS AND RHYTHMIC SOUNDS, tantalizing tastes and exotic smells of old New Orleans linger with visitors long after they have left the Queen City of the South. For some—and for many who live there and others who have moved away—the languid city grabs a piece of their hearts and never lets go. It is not the City That Care Forgot because of its abundant good times during pre-Lenten Carnival alone, though New Orleans holds more parades and festivals than there are days in the year. New Orleanians parade at funerals and weddings, march in honor of saints and Saints' football victories, and throw exuberant parties to celebrate jazz, blues, French Quarter ambience, and on the slightest of other pretexts. Friday or Saturday at midnight, when lights are flicking off up and down the Mississippi River, and lonesome freight trains are cutting into the darkness throughout the South, the night is young on rollicking Bourbon Street, where strangers walk the streets with paper cups of beer and plastic souvenir glasses of sweet hurricane cocktails, toasting life and one another. Music is everywhere in New Orleans. It filters out of jazz joints and blues clubs, out of churches and even a Voodoo museum, and echoes down the streets as a brass band prances past or a street-corner musician wails on his saxophone. Though New Orleans is a relatively poor, often steamy, sometimes inefficient, some would say decadent place, preoccupied more with its annual Carnival than with affairs of state, most residents and visitors have grown to love it that way.

The Crescent City—thus named because the Mississippi River coils so acutely past town that the sun actually rises over the West Bank in spots—has the saucy ambience of a Caribbean outpost blessed with American amenities. New Orleans is Latin *mañana*, Italian zest, French *joie de vivre*, African-American effervescence, Uptown Creole pomp, all stirred with a dash of southern indolence and a sprinkle of tropical raindrops into a savory cultural gumbo unmatched in the nation. *Laissez les bon temps rouler*—Let the Good Times Roll—is a way of life.

Originally overwhelmingly Catholic in the Protestant South, and virtually surrounded by water, New Orleans delights in its idiosyncrasies. As New Orleans storyteller, racetrack railbird, and television personality Ronnie Virgets once put it, "We enjoy simmering in our isolation." What are those idiosyncrasies? In New Orleans, tombs are aboveground "cities of the dead," owing to soil that is little more than compacted sand. Canal Street never had a canal. Two of its most famous mayors were named "Moon" and "Dutch"; one of its most famous writers went by "Pie," and a great musician by "Pud."

New Orleanians ignore the surgeon general in droves. They smoke, drink alcohol and strong coffee made stouter still by the ground chicory herb, and jauntily eat things that are bad for them: fried oysters, praline candy that is little more than pure crystallized sugar, mayonnaise on "po-boy" sandwiches, muffalettas stacked with cold cuts and oily olive mix. Only begrudgingly did the city give up a drink called absinthe, a green-colored, anise-tasting concoction laced with an addictive additive called "wormwood" that caused delusions and was so powerful that it pitted the marble counters of establishments that served it.

Of course, New Orleans seems destined to be colorful. Peaceful Choctaw Indians inhabited the swampy surroundings when the remnants of Hernando de Soto's party passed by in retreat from an expedition up the Mississippi River in the mid-1500s. More than a century later, René Robert Cavelier, Sieur de La Salle, sailed the length of the river from the Great Lakes, came upon the fertile land near the Gulf of Mexico, and claimed it—and all of the territory drained by the Mississippi—for France. He named it all "Louisiana" in honor of the Sun King, Louis XIV. Two

James Michalopoulos was a struggling New Orleans street artist and muralist before his unconventional take on the city's architecture caught fire. He now has three galleries in the New Orleans area, and his distinctive paintings and set designs are in demand around the world.

Today Bayou Saint John, running through the heart of town, is lined with pleasant homes and manicured parks. But it was once a cluttered commercial corridor for activities such as boatbuilding at the old Spanish shipyards.

French Canadians—Pierre Le Moyne, Sieur d'Iberville and his brother, Jean Baptiste Le Moyne, Sieur de Bienville—founded the first settlement, *La Nouvelle Orléans*, for which each is remembered with a street name in the French Quarter. German peasants soon joined them. They took French surnames; Webers became Fabres, Zweigs became LaBranches, and so forth. New Orleans was a French city until 1762 when Louis XV simply gave Louisiana to his Bourbon cousin, Charles III of Spain. The Spanish were nearby, as Spanish Florida extended to the present-day Louisiana parishes north of Lake Pontchartrain. When the first Spanish governor arrived to take charge, he was unceremoniously turned away, but Spanish rule eventually settled in for four decades. The Spaniards' exuberant architecture took hold, and place names were changed; visitors can see them today inset in tile in French Quarter sidewalks.

On another whim, Spain ceded Louisiana back to France in 1803. But the *tricolor* did not fly for long. By year's end, Napoleon Bonaparte sold the entire territory to Thomas Jefferson, president of the United States. The price was $11 million in U.S. bonds, for which the young nation received 831,000 square miles of land stretching to present-day Montana and doubling the country's size. New Orleans was already a yeasty city of French and Spanish aristocrats, black slaves from Haiti and Africa, free blacks, white adventurers called "Kaintucks" who had floated rafts down the Mississippi River, rich American sugar planters, and mixed-race "Creoles of color." French was the everyday language, with English-speaking Americans consigned to their own section above Canal Street. This would later become the genteel Garden District, the winter home of wealthy plantation owners and their families. A number of Acadian exiles from Canada who did not follow other "Cajuns" to Southwest Louisiana also lived in the city.

By the Civil War, Louisiana had in effect become three states in one: polyglot, Catholic New

Orleans and surroundings; Catholic Acadiana; and Protestant central and northern parishes. Tensions among the regions prompted the state legislature to move the capital from New Orleans to Baton Rouge, which was wedged among them all in the center of the state. By 1860, New Orleans was a thriving city of 168,000. It was the center of the cotton and sugar South, and—despite its tolerant traditions—slaves were auctioned off daily under the rotunda of the opulent Saint Louis Hotel as lunch was served all around. In Congo Square, a small plain surrounded by a picket fence in the shadow of the city's former ramparts, slaves performed tribal and Voodoo dances for the amusement and amazement of white audiences.

Owing to its strategic position, New Orleans was an early target in the Civil War. The city was easily captured by Admiral David Farragut's menacing gunboats in 1862, and was soon occupied by fifteen thousand Union troops. Their commander was the detested General Ben "Spoons" Butler, so called because of his penchant for appropriating residents' silver. The women of the city went one better, calling him "Beast" Butler because he declared that any New Orleans lady showing disrespect to the occupying forces would be treated as a common prostitute.

Along the way to its reluctant accommodation with the rest of America in the late twentieth century, New Orleans battled floods, rampant corruption at home and the political machines of Huey P. Long and other Louisiana governors in Baton Rouge, and epidemics of yellow fever. The impact of the fever can be discerned in the city's graveyards, where row after row of victims are entombed, some in multi-level "apartment buildings" for the dead. New Orleans became one of the nation's first service economies, providing workboats, crews, supplies, and later helicopters to offshore oil rigs—and began to add hotels and other facilities to court the tourist dollar. Big chains like Hilton, Sheraton, and Marriott avoided the city until

Without the earthen levee along the Mississippi River— and mighty pumps— much of New Orleans would be under water. From warehouses all along the levee, dockworkers loaded cargo such as these casks of sugar.

The "Streetcar Named Desire" once rattled down Royal Street through the French Quarter on its way to the Desire neighborhood. So did Mardi Gras floats, until they were banned as fire hazards.

the passage of the Civil Rights Act of 1964, but they made up for their late start by building giant facilities downtown. The 1984 Louisiana World Exposition—an artistic success but a financial disappointment—prompted the construction of even more hotels, which, combined with a gigantic new convention center that sprang directly from a fair pavilion, cemented New Orleans as a top convention destination.

Almost nowhere in this "checkerboard city," where the races live in close proximity in every part of town, will you hear the sultry southern accents that actors affect in movies set in New Orleans. The real endemic accent is more Brooklyn than bayou, as working-class "yats" (the term "yat" comes from the colorful greeting "Hey, where y'at?") go to "woik" changing "earl," or "makin' groceries" at the Schwegmann's store, sometimes even on a "Sundi." Chartres Street in the French Quarter is pronounced "Charters." Burgundy is "BurGUNdy." Calliope is "CALee-owp." Visitors and Yankee transplants call the city New ORlins. Musicians like the rhyme of New OrLEENS. But the local preference is NewWALyunz, except in highbrow circles Uptown, where the word gets an extra syllable: New OR-li-unz.

Tourists are often surprised not to hear French spoken everywhere on the streets. To their surprise, Italian-Americans are the largest white ethnic group in Metropolitan New Orleans. Italians, or more precisely, Sicilian peasants, first came to New Orleans after the American Civil War as almost indentured servants, replacing departed black fieldhands. They labored for fifty cents a day on Louisiana's sugar plantations. Through hard work and frugality, Italians came to dominate truck farming, the import and export trade, and the retail and wholesale grocery business. By 1937, there were six hundred grocery stores in Greater New Orleans owned by Italians, and almost 80 percent of the "French" Quarter was Italian-owned. "Little Palermo," as the

Quarter was known to some, included an Italian Roman Catholic church, the big Monteleone Hotel, a boxing gym that produced light heavyweight Willie Pastrano and other champions, Italian ice companies, and "French Market" farmers' stands that were almost exclusively Italian. Companies like Progresso Foods and Standard Fruit grew into giant international corporations. The first jazz recording in America in 1917 featured New Orleans trumpeter Nick LaRocca—the son of an immigrant Sicilian shoemaker—and his Original Dixieland Jass Band; singer and trumpeter Louis Prima and dozens of other top musicians also came out of New Orleans. When a way was found to sink pilings into the city's soupy soil, it was Italian-American developers who built the first high-rise towers. While many families have moved to the suburbs, the Italian influence is recalled at the American-Italian Museum in the Warehouse District, in a Festa D'Italia that coincides with Columbus Day in October, and in Saint Joseph's Day celebrations each March. Saint Joseph's Day honors the patron saint of Sicily. Families decorate altars with religious icons, as well as lavish spreads of cakes, cookies, and other homemade specialties that are later donated to the poor.

New Orleans has also had a subtle Latin flavor almost since its founding. Most early French traffic passed through Santo Domingo—part Spanish, part French in its culture—on the way to New Orleans. Coffee and fruit companies with huge plantations in Central and South America got started in New Orleans, and the city was the first "Gateway to the Americas" before being supplanted by Miami and Houston. New Orleans sugar barons had ties to Cuba. Louisiana and Venezuelan oil companies shared technologies. New Orleans was the favorite destination for wealthy Latinos in search of fun or medical treatment. And wealthy Latin business leaders (and more than one dictator) built winter homes in the Garden District. Today the metropolitan

Originally a military training ground, Jackson Square became a public pleasure ground and the center of Spanish administration. The Louisiana Purchase was ratified in the Cabildo to the left of Saint Louis Cathedral.

Metairie Cemetery, west of town, became the largest "City of the Dead." New Orleans's watery soil would not permit underground burial. In tinier neighborhood cemeteries, families and yellow fever victims were interred in humbler "accommodations."

area is home to more than one hundred fifty thousand Hispanics, including more Hondurans than live in all but two cities in that Central American nation. There are no *barrios*, however; Latinos—including young professionals working in shipping and import-export businesses, medicine, and banking—have been assimilated into the overall population. But Latinos are not the only Spanish-speaking citizens. Long before them came *Isleños,* a few thousand Spaniards from the Canary Islands, who found work in the bayous south and east of New Orleans. The *Isleños* have maintained an antique Spanish dialect and produced several colorful business entrepreneurs.

Creole and black cultures are in full flower in New Orleans. Many Negro slaves bought their freedom in the broad-minded river city as early as 1770, and other free blacks emigrated from the Caribbean. The community of "free people of color"—including Creole children of French-Negro mixing—was the largest in America (larger than New York's) by the Civil War. Following decades of racial segregation and restrictive Jim Crow laws analogous to others throughout the South, Creoles emerged as New Orleans's political elite. Other African Americans found success through music, especially jazz. No one has yet pinned down the exact moment that jazz was born, though there is agreement that at least one of its roots traces to the "talking drums" that slaves brought from West Africa. The first band known to have played jazz was Buddy Bolden's African-American ensemble in New Orleans in 1895. The musicians called it "ratty music," "gut bucket," or "ragtime." But this improvisational, unscripted style of music, where musicians often do not read music but memorize their parts and embellish them in wild solos, was quite different from the intricate ragtime of W. C. Handy and others up the Mississippi River in Saint Louis and Chicago. In truth, many black musicians were and are superb reading musicians, but the "faking" style became popular with the rise of the Bolden band and ultimately forced skilled players in some cases to "unskill" themselves and learn how to improvise. In the years immediately following World War I, the terms "jazz," "creole," and "Dixieland" were used interchangeably by white and black New Orleans bands alike. Later, "jazz" became associated with African-American groups, with "Dixieland" thought of as a white imitation. Talent, and not race, is the overriding qualification for membership in most great New Orleans jazz bands today.

When visitors buy an album of New Orleans music and look carefully at the small print, they often find that it was recorded in New York or Nashville and distributed out of Los Angeles or New York. Though the Crescent City has rich musical raw materials (and a fanatical following in Japan and parts of Europe), it has a minuscule share of the booming global entertainment market. The wildly successful Neville Brothers hit it big by opening for the Rolling Stones on tour. Pianist Harry Connick Jr. gained fame from a sound track to the movie *When Harry Met Sally*. New Orleans performers like Dr. John and the Marsalis family of musicians have been famous for years because of hits recorded outside New Orleans. One reason is that the city's conservative bankers preferred to invest in Louisiana crops like cotton and sugar, and later in oil and gas, rather than get involved in the risky music business. Even though tourism became a huge industry in New Orleans after World War II, music was viewed as it is in underdeveloped countries—as a quaint part of neighborhood culture, but not as a viable industry. For decades, New Orleans did not even keep a simple registry of saxophonists, drummers, and other players. Musicians often played without a contract, kept sloppy financial records, and did little to promote their bands. New Orleans supported only a few tiny record labels, and talent

Encouraged to locate in their own section apart from the ruling French, wealthy Americans built lavish homes along Saint Charles Avenue, which followed the winding Mississippi River away from the French Quarter.

that somehow snared the national spotlight was soon snatched away by one of the big New York or Los Angeles labels.

But New Orleans is determined to change all this. The city's music commission has aggressively supported movies, music videos, and albums made in town; built a giant post-production studio; and established both a Black Music Hall of Fame and a historical jazz park. And the state legislature in Baton Rouge cooperated by passing a law that set up a capital corporation to invest in small businesses. Much of the $100 million in risk capital raised in the first few years of the 1990s went directly into New Orleans music ventures. The attention paid to New Orleans music is welcome, but authorities like Bruce Raeburn, director of the renowned Tulane University Jazz Archive, warn of a potential downside: national exposure and dollars could slicken the gritty street sound of New Orleans music in the name of selling albums and music videos, thus destroying the ingredients that make New Orleans music unique.

The arts in New Orleans are not confined to music clubs, the New Orleans Museum of Art in City Park, the Contemporary Arts Center, or the Saenger Performing Arts Center. At a most unconventional high school, the New Orleans Center for the Creative Arts—or NOCCA—one of the first schools of its kind in the country, energetic young people study music, visual arts, dance, acting, and writing. Inside, ragged riffs of music leak over a transom above a classroom door, and one can hear dancers shuffling and poets reciting down the hall. Students—who must pass auditions and several interviews to be accepted—dash everywhere, carrying paint pots and play scripts and slide trombones, and what few adults one sees are more likely to be dressed in Bermuda shorts and a T-shirt than a dress or a suit and tie. Drama students study global theater, including African ritual, as well as a spate of great American plays. The NOCCA students have several role models, including graduates Branford and Wynton Marsalis and Harry Connick Jr.

To this crossroads of French, Spanish, Italian, African, and Anglo-Saxon cultures have come gustatory masters as well. Before the Civil War, slaves, not fancy chefs, did most of the cooking. Their ingredients were some of the finest in the world, imported into this great seaport from

Cotton was king in the South, and it was at the New Orleans Cotton Exchange where prices were set and deals arranged. New Orleans's 1884 world's fair was called the Industrial & Cotton Centennial Exposition.

France, Spain, Italy, and the Caribbean Islands; caught in nearby bayous and the Gulf; or grown in Louisiana and Mississippi fields. Many of the legendary restaurants of New Orleans started as humble extentions of corner grocery stores. The food was so delicious, it drew an international following. "Cajun chef" Paul Prudhomme, for instance, became a celebrity with his cookbooks and videotapes. Prudhomme added zest and simplicity to delicate Creole dishes; and he set off a nationwide craze by "blackening"—searing with ample spices—redfish and chicken. A New Orleans meal became an event in itself. A table at Arnaud's, Antoine's, Gallatoire's, Pascal's Manale, Commander's Palace, or the original Ruth's Chris steakhouse became a prize for lucky visitors and locals alike; and "breakfast at Brennan's" turned into a lingering indulgence. New Orleans lovers even swear "Lucky Dog" frankfurters served from French Quarter pushcarts, "king cake" iced Mardi Gras streudels, and summertime sno-cones ladled with sticky, flavored syrups are a cut above such common fare in other cities.

Ornate wrought-iron balconies, the triple spires of Saint Louis Cathedral in Jackson Square, and the streetcars that rattle through the

city are three famous symbols of Old New Orleans. By 1900, streetcar service was already sixty-five years old. Horse-drawn cars, steam-powered streetcars, and even trolleys powered by ammonia engines had served the city. By 1902, electrified streetcars were running out Saint Charles Avenue to what was then a resort area called Carrollton at a huge bend in the river. "All one has to do is to repose comfortably upon a springy cane seat and view the landscape as he goes along," read a pamphlet called *Around the Saint Charles Belt.* "Several such trips will serve to leave a lasting and very pleasant impression upon the mind." Back when the city had more than six hundred operating streetcars, the Desire line—made famous by playwright Tennessee Williams—ran through the heart of the French Quarter. One by one, however, the streetcar lines gave way to buses, until only those plying the "neutral ground" (the grassy median strip) of Saint Charles Avenue line were left. Its thirty-five steel cars, painted a drab Army green and powered by sixty-five-horsepower engines front and back, became the nation's only moving National Landmark. They run past opulent Uptown mansions and two of New Orleans's pre-eminent universities, Loyola and Tulane—which are separated by only a skimpy hedge on campuses across from Audubon Park. The latter school, founded in 1834 as the public Medical College of Louisiana, the south's first medical school, was reorganized in 1884 as a private institution named for benefactor Paul Tulane. With the development of the Riverwalk shopping complex at the end of Poydras Street in the late 1980s, the regional transit authority put six more streetcars, painted red, in service along the river. The line connects the convention center, the Riverwalk, and the wharves and coffee stands across from Jackson Square in the Quarter. The city also retained Car 453, one of the original "Streetcars Named Desire." It was kept for a time near the old U.S. Mint near the French Market but was eventually retired

Canal Street was the city's busy commercial and transportation hub, the original dividing line between French and American sections. Despite its name, the street never had a canal.

to an obscure car barn. Still, streetcar aficionados from all over the world manage to find it, usually after a ride on the oldest continuously operating streetcar system in the world.

While streetcars are a curiosity, New Orleans's Carnival, a fantasy world unmatched in North America, is a multimillion-dollar draw. In a festive ritual first brought to New Orleans from nearby Mobile, Alabama, in 1857, weeks of parades and costume balls culminate on Mardi Gras, or "Fat Tuesday"—so called because it is the last shot at gluttony and intemperance before somber Ash Wednesday and the beginning of Lent. Masked members of (usually secret) societies and social clubs called "krewes" ride on elaborate floats (now pulled by tractors instead of mules), dispensing beads and other trinkets to throngs of revelers. "Throw me somethin', mistah" is the battle cry of the savvy parade-goer. While Carnival can get rowdy on Bourbon Street, it is also a family affair. On the Mardi Gras holiday, parents dress up in imaginative costumes, lay out picnic spreads on Napoleon Avenue and Saint Charles Avenue neutral grounds, prop small children on stepladders for a good view (and a better chance at catching beads and doubloons), and enjoy the day. Zulu, a zany black krewe, parades in the morning, throwing painted coconuts and other treasures. The last daytime parade is ruled by Rex, king of Carnival. Then come "truck parades," less elaborate, but often more original and clever. They are rolling displays of mirth on one hundred or more flatbed trucks decorated by neighborhood groups from all over the city; riders throw used beads and other trifles from years past, dress in simple and often outlandish costumes, and laugh along with some of the hundreds of thousands of tourists who jam the city. America's greatest free show becomes more elaborate each year, particularly on the Saturday night before Mardi Gras, when the Krewe of Endymion parades at night on outrageous double- and triple-decker lighted floats. Some old-line krewes such as Comus—which

For generations, Café Du Monde has offered chicory-laced café au lait and hot, hole-less French donuts called beignets at all hours. The café has since moved up Decatur Street from this French Market location.

Antoine's Restaurant staff posed to mark the 150th anniversary of the gracious old restaurant in 1990. Its classic Creole dinner menu is almost as long as the list of distinguished visitors who have enjoyed "dinner at Antoine's."

first brought Carnival to New Orleans—hold coronation balls but ceased parading after rancorous city council hearings in the early 1990s in which they were chastised for not accepting minority members.

At the beginning of the twentieth century, New Orleans had four times as many people as Atlanta, seven times as many as Houston, and more than two hundred times as many residents as the sleepy little beach community of Miami. In the ensuing years the Big Easy coasted along, basking in its rich history and culture, and enjoying the bounty of its oil-and-gas and tourism industries while those other metropolitan areas rocketed past drowsy New Orleans to become significant international business centers. Few among New Orleans's entrenched elite who ran the banks and oil, seafood, cotton, rice, coffee, fruit, and sulphur companies took much notice until the mid-1980s, when domestic oil prices plummeted from forty dollars to ten dollars a barrel, smacking the Louisiana economy harder than had the Great Depression of the 1930s. Other businesses spiraled downward as well, and total employment of all kinds fell by eight percent between 1981 and 1987. New Orleans learned the hard way that once a city loses international business, it is difficult to get it back.

The "oil bust" forced the Crescent City to practically re-invent its economy. Officials in Orleans Parish (New Orleans) and eight surrounding parishes responded by forming a new organization called MetroVision, committed to turning the region into an aggressive and interdependent economic machine. Greater New Orleans already included blue-collar Saint Bernard Parish and wealthier Jefferson Parish—where the suburb of Metairie had its own office towers and shopping centers to go with its stunning residential enclaves. In the 1990s, parishes in the old Spanish Florida, north of the world's longest concrete bridge, the twenty-four-mile-

Although the French Quarter has always been known for stronger libations, a deliveryman pulls up with a shipment of milk for the Restaurant de la Louisiane *in the 1890s. Note Iberville Street's rough cobblestones.*

long Lake Pontchartrain Causeway, experienced phenomenal growth. What had once been sparsely settled piney woods became hot real estate, as commuters—and telecommuters—gobbled up lots on the relatively safe, quiet, and cool "North Shore."

MetroVision's first order of business was to diversify the regional economy by targeting growth industries like the medical-supply businesses that serve New Orleans's vast hospital community. The second priority was to purge the smug satisfaction at having perhaps the nation's greatest concentration of natural resources, and to concentrate on adding value to those resources. Instead of just catching shrimp and shipping them abroad in bulk, for instance, area governments lent a hand to businesses that process and package the shellfish. And MetroVision began selling New Orleans's business potential by citing the example of Freeport-McMoRan. The giant oil-and-mineral exploration company moved its corporate headquarters from New York's Wall Street to Poydras Street in New Orleans in the mid-1980s, saving more than $300 million in operating costs as a result.

The Port of New Orleans, once the nation's busiest, was caught dozing when the shipping industry embraced containerization over bulk cargoes in the 1970s. Awakened, the port spent $250 million to modernize, with an eye toward capitalizing on the lower tariffs that came with the signing of the North American Free Trade Agreement. The port shifted focus from Pacific Rim imports that had moved to containers to emerging markets in Latin America and Europe. Both the port and the city as a whole also began to exploit New Orleans's strong African-American community by developing new trade ties to predominantly black countries like Haiti and South Africa.

The city had a more fundamental obstacle to increasing foreign trade, however. How could it overcome its image as a party town and prove that it was serious about business? MetroVision used the example of Phoenix, which had been thought of as a great place to play golf in January. That Arizona metropolis proved itself a good year-round business location and dramatically changed its economic growth rate. New Orleans also began to court international tourists as never before. The city pointed out that few places in the Western Hemisphere flew the French, Spanish, and United States flags as it does, are as distinctive culturally and architecturally, or operate at such an easygoing, tourist-friendly pace. In order to rise to the level of a truly world-class city, New Orleans also squarely faced two other image problems: rising crime and poor school performance. The city brought in a reform-minded police commissioner who began the fight against crime in-house by weeding out widespread corruption in his own department. And MetroVision began a model school program in which at least one high school in each parish works with local industries like medicine and banking. The curriculum in these schools reflects skills that will be used in the workplace, plus practical work experience through internships.

New Orleans in the 1990s also rekindled its longstanding ties with Latin America. New mayor Marc Morial was one of only two U.S. mayors to attend the Summit of the Americas in Miami. And he appointed an assistant for international trade, charged with recapturing a piece of the economic and technological revolution in Central and South America. MetroVision organized trade shows and began an all-out effort called "Inter-Cambio 2000," aimed at identifying buyers for New Orleans's goods in Mexico, Central America, and the north and west coasts of South America. The effort faced many obstacles: Unlike Houston, New Orleans has a small manufacturing base. Unlike Miami, it's not a large international finance center. And New Orleans has just a fraction of the direct air and passenger service to key Latin American trade centers. But MetroVision pointed out that it is also the perfect trading partner—close by, with a Spanish and French (and Catholic) history, Caribbean flavor, Napoleonic legal code, and a relaxed way of doing business. And three fourths of the United States can be reached from New Orleans via the Mississippi River and its tributaries.

Signs of a turnaround abounded all over town. Upriver from the French Quarter, in the once-seedy Warehouse District, old brick buildings were turned into tony restaurants and loft apartments. New Orleans's new convention center and the Riverwalk were impressive legacies of the 1984 Louisiana World's Fair, which first turned the crumbling Warehouse District into desirable real estate. Orleans Parish undertook another economic initiative, giving new meaning to the catchphrase "Let the good times roll" when it voted to allow casino gambling, first in modest riverboat casinos and then in what was planned as the largest gambling palace in the world. New Orleans talked Harrah's Corporation into demolishing the old Rivergate exhibition hall on the edge of Canal Street and replacing it with a megacasino that was to be a veritable gaming theme park—with five giant, themed gambling halls (including a sinking pirate's ship) under one roof. Harrah's paid the State of Louisiana $125 million just for the right to be the state's exclusive land-based casino, and it estimated that the complex would bring in one million new tourists, thousands of jobs, and millions of new tax dollars each year. Harrah's then spent $41 million to renovate the 1930s-vintage municipal auditorium in the rough Tremé neighborhood into a temporary casino, while construction was completed on the monolith downtown. But catastrophic problems arose: the temporary casino dramatically underperformed and was closed, and construction was halted on the megacasino in midstream. After high-level negotiations and threats to transfer the rights to another company, Harrah's and the city agreed to a scaled-down version of the giant casino. All the

The organ grinder was a draw for old and young alike. Today, the French Quarter is filled with sounds of street musicians, as well as jazz and zydeco spilling out of Bourbon Street clubs.

while, Mayor Morial made it clear that he and his constituents had no desire to turn New Orleans into a "gambling destination," but that gaming would be another valued ingredient to complement the cultural tourism, food, and architecture that are the city's primary attractions.

Gaming halls built by outsiders were just one example of a growing, and often begrudging, homogenization of the New Orleans culture. Local institutions like powerful WWL television and radio, owned by the Catholic Church, were sold to outsiders. Jax beer went out of business, its former brewery now full of upscale shops; and Dixie Beer sales lag behind those of several national brands. Even McDonald's "Golden Arches" and a Hard Rock Café found their way into the French Quarter. Big local department stores like the D. H. Holmes Company closed or were bought by out-of-town chains. Storyville's Basin Street jazz halls and risqué bawdy houses are barely a memory, replaced by bleak housing projects. Slot machines, once as common as ceiling fans, are long gone. Though clinging stubbornly to its remaining anachronisms, New Orleans is at last becoming a fully American city. Still, grumped Ronnie Virgets, "Newcomers come and make their changes, and in the process of searching out quaintness, they threaten it."

These changes led to growing disillusionment about the city on the part of many residents. Reacting to a survey by the Young Leadership Council in the 1990s that found whites, blacks, Hispanics, old and young people alike reporting more negative than positive feelings about New Orleans and its quality of life, Ti Martin, owner of the Palace Café on Canal Street, helped organize a boosterism campaign with the slogan "Proud to Call It Home." "I just was frustrated by the feeling that 'You can't change that.' It's one thing to be cynical about the [often woeful] Saints, but quite another to be cynical about the city, its politicians, and its future." The campaign featured its own upbeat theme song, written by famous New Orleans composer Allen Toussaint. The song begins: "We've got good reason to love this beautiful city—the jewel of the Mississippi River. This precious gem is unique in all the land—the Queen of the South: New Orleans. The world comes knocking at the door. She says, 'Yes, y'all come on in.'" The Proud to Call It Home campaign pointed out the boomlet in oil-related jobs, the building of the nation's largest convention center, and the fact that New Orleans boasted the second-lowest cost of living of any American city.

These initiatives, a slow rebound in the oil economy, and a surge in tourism brought an almost palpable increase in confidence throughout the city. But modest prosperity brought yet another challenge—how to manage growth and diversification, while retaining the city's character, beauty, architecture, and ambience.

In the movie *The Big Easy*, set in New Orleans, the hero and heroine are at one point running for their lives. They race from a typical New Orleans neighborhood of wrought-iron balconies and long, thin "shotgun" houses directly into the swamp to hide. For such a thing to happen in real life, the characters would have a long run indeed. There are a few Mississippi River spillways near New Orleans, but nearby swamps have been drained. To take a swamp tour, one must travel more than one hundred fifty miles to Cajun Country. Most Great River Road plantation homes, likewise, are many miles away in central Louisiana, nearer to Baton Rouge than New Orleans. Nonetheless, much as distant Valley Forge is a staple of a Philadelphia visit—and

Rex, king of Carnival—and Lord of Misrule!—reigns in 1893. The flowing locks are a wig, for businessman John Poitevent wore his hair short and well-groomed in his dealings away from the cheering crowds.

Rex 1940 stops at the Boston Club, where he will meet his queen. According to Carnival lore, Rex's father is Old King Cole, his mother Terpsichore, the Greek muse of dancing and song.

Lexington and Concord battle sites are an essential part of the Boston experience—swamp and mansion tours are favorite side trips on a visit to New Orleans. So are trips to amazing Avery Island, the beautiful egret sanctuary and home to the famous Tabasco hot-sauce factory near New Iberia.

But there are beauty and history aplenty in Greater New Orleans itself—in verdant Audubon and City parks, Uptown and in the Garden District, along Bayou Saint John, in botanical wonderlands like the Longue Vue Gardens in Metairie, and in the French Quarter. In Jackson Square alone, visitors can take in the Saint Louis Cathedral and its flanking buildings, the Cabildo and the Presbytere, both part of the Louisiana State Museum. The Cabildo, which was the seat of Spanish rule and the place where the Louisiana Purchase agreement was signed in 1803, retraces the exploration of Louisiana and its history through Reconstruction. The Presbytere, which once housed state courts, is now a showcase of Louisiana culture of the twentieth century.

On a foggy morning outside Saint Louis Cathedral, one can almost picture oneself running to the levee to greet the steamboat. Even ramshackle shotgun houses and tiny cafés are fascinating links to a romantic past. Where else in America could a cheap but divine dish like red beans and rice with andouille sausage, once a washerwoman's Monday-pot meal, be a cultural icon? New Orleans still hypnotizes as no other American city can. More than five hundred song titles mention New Orleans, and uncounted thousands more visit the city somewhere in their lyrics. Painters and photographers are as thick as Louisiana mudbugs (crawfish), and writers flock in to soak up the hedonism. As James Agee wrote: "New Orleans is stirring, rattling, sliding faintly in the fragrance of the enormous riches of its lust." There's no doubt about it; once New Orleans gets in your blood, it's there to stay.

Tile signs identifying Spanish names for streets and landmarks such as Jackson Square (above) can be found throughout the French Quarter. Even though Louisiana Territory was Spanish for only forty-one years, much of the architecture of the Quarter is Spanish, because earlier French buildings were destroyed by fire. The 1799 Cabildo (right) in Jackson Square was the courthouse and center of the last years of Spanish colonial administration. The Cabildo was later home to the Louisiana State Supreme Court, where Plessy v. Ferguson and other landmark cases were argued. Now part of the Louisiana State Museum, the Cabildo houses artifacts from colonial and early Louisiana state history.

New Orleans's best-known landmark, the 1794 Saint Louis Cathedral (left) is America's oldest cathedral. It was a gift to the city from Spanish nobleman Don Andres Almonester y Roxas, who built it "on condition that mass would be said every Sunday in perpetuity after his death for the repose of his soul." Indeed, although tourists often just briefly peek inside the cathedral (opposite), full masses are still held there every day. Clark Mills's equestrian statue of Andrew Jackson, hero of the Battle of New Orleans, is a copy of those in Washington, D.C., and Nashville, Tennessee. Benjamin Butler, the detested commander of occupying Federal forces, ordered the inscription, "The Union must and shall be preserved" carved into its pedestal during the Civil War.

A buggy tour (right) is a leisurely way to enjoy the sights of the French Quarter. Tour guides are exuberant storytellers, though the accuracy of their tales varies greatly. Buggies line up in front of Jackson Square, and others, like this Mid-City Carriage, give customized tours through the Quarter and elsewhere in the city.

Concern over the treatment of mules (above), especially in New Orleans's steamy summers, led to the placement of drinking troughs and strict inspection of the animals' care. The clip-clop of mules' hooves, mingled with distant music and laughter, endures as a "sound souvenir" of pleasurable visits to the romantic old city.

Voodoo tours, readings, drum and chant rituals, and artifacts of the great Voodoo queen, Marie Laveau, are staples at the New Orleans Historic Voodoo Museum in the French Quarter. Visitors can get their own good-luck *gris-gris* bags of herbs and oils and arrange for spooky tours of swamp country. They can even stay overnight in the "Voodoo Arms" apartments overlooking the museum courtyard. The Vieux Carré is also the place to find fortune tellers like "Madame Michael," who reads palms and tarot cards in front of the Presbytere on Jackson Square. The streets beneath the square's Pontalba Apartments—built by a baroness in 1849—are also lined with artists who sketch visitors in chalk, charcoal, or pencil. Others offer watercolors, oils, and prints of French Quarter scenes.

Delicate china masks (opposite), available in French Quarter shops and at weekend bazaars at the French Market, are a favorite New Orleans souvenir. Even life-size street mannequins (left)— usually not for sale— are not an unusual sight. But then, surprises abound around every turn in the kitschy Vieux Carré. Other keepsakes on the "low end" of expense range from sugary praline candy to glasses left after trying a "hurricane," the city's signature sweet alcoholic drink. Visitors also carry home strong ground New Orleans coffee, bags of beignet mix, and even crawfish protected in dry ice. The culinary experience in one's own kitchen, however, rarely matches the ambience of the dreamy Quarter. "High end" souvenirs are available in the many art galleries and antique shops along Royal Street.

Until a world-class aquarium opened in the Riverwalk, the shopping pavilion along the Mississippi River on the site of the 1984 Louisiana World's Fair, New Orleans offered few attractions for children. In a way, though, the entire city is an amusement park. Street clowns, like balloon maker Darryl Poché (above), are everywhere. And kids as well as adults can get a fascinating behind-the-scenes look at year-round preparations for the monthlong Carnival celebration by visiting Blaine Kern's Mardi Gras World, across the river from the French Quarter on the West Bank. Here, artisans like Brian Bush (opposite) touch up and restore the hundreds of giant papier-mâché and fiberglass figures—such as Godzilla, Peter Pan, the Creature from the Black Lagoon, and the heads of famous figures like George Washington, Marilyn Monroe, and Frankenstein's monster—that roll in Carnival parades.

French Quarter mimes, like Erod Newton (opposite), are a study in body control. Like the royal guards at London's Buckingham Palace, these human statues delight in outlasting good-natured tormentors. Less flashy mimes have even been mistaken for sculptures. Few street characters' costumes compare, however, to the extravagant ensembles that appear at Carnival. Allen Little (above) is the captain of the "Mystic Krewe of Perseus," one of several Carnival organizations that parades through the streets of New Orleans, surrounding suburbs, and elsewhere in South Louisiana. A krewe captain gets much of the work organizing each year's parade and other events—and little of the glory that a king or queen receives. Still, Little gets to pull out one of his dozen or so elaborate vestments for a day of mirth with fellow Perseus members once a year.

*Mardi Gras is often
confused with
Carnival. The latter
is a monthlong
festival of parades
and balls leading
up to Mardi Gras—
"Fat Tuesday"—
the last day of indul-
gence before solemn
Ash Wednesday. On
Mardi Gras, select
Carnival krewes and
hundreds of thou-
sands of merrymakers
dress up, whoop it up,
and soak up the spec-
tacle. "Dr. Rose"—
Tom Perkins—
(right), is a year-
round French Quarter
fixture, but these
unidentified charac-
ters (opposite) are
fixed up just for
Mardi Gras. On
that one day, nearly
everybody but police,
medics, convenience-
store workers, and
clean-up krewes has
the day off for fun.
Hijinks border on
debauchery in the
French Quarter, but
elsewhere it's a day
when families picnic
and youngsters beg
for trinkets from
passing parades.*

Bourbon Street on Mardi Gras (left) is a sea of revelry on the street and in balconies above. A walk from Canal Street to the first break in the crowd can take an hour. On any Friday or Saturday night, it's as much fun watching tourists watch the inebriates, uninhibited dancers, and moon-howlers as watching these characters themselves. One of the oldest and most popular Carnival parading organiza-tions is the Krewe of Zulu, whose members (above) roll on Mardi Gras morning. Zulu's "throws" include prized painted Zulu coconuts. Not just on Mardi Gras but also year round in Bourbon Street clubs like the Maison Bourbon (overleaf), Dixieland jazz is the traditional sound of the city. This happy music is characterized by extemporaneous riffs by each band member.

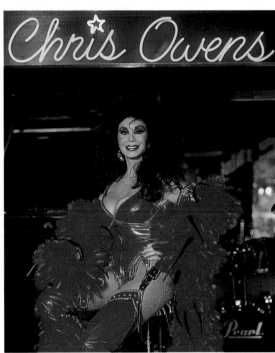

Except in the wee hours, an occasional Sunday morning, or a rare moment before dinnertime when the city seems to take a breath before another wild evening, Bourbon Street (left) is rarely deserted. Tawdry in spots, with ample striptease clubs and adult shops, the feel-good center of "The City that Care Forgot" has a surprising number of good hotels, oyster bars, jazz clubs, and restaurants. In its lower reaches, there are even several blocks of quiet row houses. For a generation, the street's most famous performer and goodwill ambassador has been saucy chanteuse Chris Owens (above), who delights crowds at her club with a rousing—and entirely tasteful—show.

"I've always wanted to play on Bourbon Street," jokes legendary New Orleans pianist Ronnie Kole (opposite). Kole did play Bourbon Street, not literally on the pavement as he does here, but in his own club for years, and once a month since then in the Mystic Den of the Royal Sonesta Hotel. Kole, a classically trained showman who has performed for presidents and popes, slides seamlessly from rollicking boogie-woogie to somber, contemplative numbers. He now tours the world as often as he plays in New Orleans. Street musicians like Hack Bartholomew (top right) play an integral part in the sound of the Crescent City as well. So do small ensembles like performers at the popular jazz brunch (bottom right) at Royal Street's Court of Two Sisters.

Owen Brennan grew up in the poor "Irish Channel" neighborhood early in this century. He was running a Bourbon Street saloon when the proprietor of a French restaurant remarked that no Irishman could successfully operate a fine eatery. Brennan proved him wrong, not only by turning "Owen Brennan's French & Creole Restaurant" into one of the city's premier dining establishments, but also by making "Breakfast at Brennan's" the nation's most famous first meal of the day. Upon his death his sister, Ella, expanded Brennan's into other Southeast locations. After a family schism, Owen Brennan's sons, "Pip," Jimmy, and Ted, (left to right, above), and their mother, Maude, assumed control of Brennan's signature Royal Street location. At Café Du Monde a couple of blocks away, veteran waiter Linus Noel (opposite) serves a humbler but also delicious fare: café au lait and beignets.

World-renowned Antoine's Restaurant is famous for its food, the attentive service of a "personal waiter," and for its amazing wine cellar (above) containing more than five thousand bottles. The oldest wine dates from 1884, the earliest brandy, 1811. Another nonpareil Creole restaurant, Arnaud's (opposite), was founded in 1918— in a building erected in 1833—by "Count" Arnaud Cazenave, a French-born bon vivant. Upon his death in 1948, his daughter, Germaine Wells, a New Orleans socialite who reigned at dozens of Mardi Gras balls, began an expansion into an astounding thirteen adjoining buildings. In an anteroom off the main dining room, many of Mrs. Wells's gowns, scepters, and crowns are displayed. Current Arnaud's proprietor Archie Casbarian, an Egyptian-born former hotelier, added what the New Orleans Times-Picayune called a "sassy sibling"—a café called Remoulade, around the corner on Bourbon Street.

French Quarter landmarks are too numerous for any buggy driver to cover in a single tour. A stately home with a beautiful courtyard (opposite) was restored by novelist Frances Parkinson Keyes in the 1940s. It was once the residence of Confederate General Pierre Gustave Toutant Beauregard, at whose direction the first shot of the Civil War was fired at Fort Sumter in 1862. The Champanel Cottage (above), now weathered, was built in 1811 as rental property by Barthelemy Champanel, a free man of color who owned a hardware store. The cottage itself was a hardware store from 1945–84. Lafitte's Blacksmith Shop (overleaf) is a quaint bar in a photogenic eighteenth-century cottage. According to legend, for which there is no evidence, pirate Jean Lafitte operated a blacksmith shop here as a front for his traffic in contraband seized from captured or wrecked ships.

The French Quarter is home to thousands of New Orleanians. Buildings at the corner of Saint Ann and Chartres streets (above), on Rampart Street on the edge of the Quarter (right), and on Chartres Street off Jackson Square (opposite), employ different architectural details, but all provide fascinating light-and-shadow studies. Inside, Vieux Carré homes (overleaf) such as that of former congresswoman Lorrine "Lindy" Boggs, are often elegant. Mrs. Boggs, daughter of onetime New Orleans mayor Chep Morrison, lives on one of the busiest—and sometimes noisiest—blocks of Bourbon Street. Her portrait as a young woman, and plates bearing the Morrison family name, grace her living room.

New Orleans has long been influenced by cultures of the Caribbean, where many wealthy French sugar planters had ties and from which thousands of slaves were brought to the city. One example is the profusion of vivid color on the façades of cottages such as the pink house on lower Bourbon Street (right). In a sense the city is rediscovering this flamboyance, for many homes had faded or deteriorated before being brightly restored. New owners carefully researched the historically correct colors of the c. 1810 "Circle Cottage" on Bourbon Street (above), for instance, before rejuvenating it. They were surprised to discover the original bright red and green hues.

New Orleans residents often enrich their homes with decorative touches, like iron grillework and festive ferns on this Royal Street balcony (above). A Bourbon Street cottage (left) employs the city's symbol— the fleur de lis. *Royal Street's Cornstalk Hotel (overleaf) is one of two New Orleans structures— the other is Uptown— enclosed by a cast-* *iron cornstalk fence entwined with iron morning-glories. The hotel was the home of Francis- Xavier Martin, first chief justice of the Louisiana Supreme Court. The story attributed inter- changeably to the two properties is that the owner's wife missed the rural scenery of the Midwest, so her con- siderate spouse ordered the cornstalk design.*

61

Except when searching for a parking place, tourists often miss seeing some classic residences in the lower French Quarter. The house (opposite) and balcony (left) are on Barracks Street. The Quarter's narrow streets and small lots did not permit owners to build fullscale neoclassical homes as they did Uptown, but many who moved into the Quarter after New Orleans became American with the Louisiana Purchase of 1803 did what they could to dress up their property. Scarce courtyard space became a prime outlet for expression of individuality in the crowded Vieux Carré, as illustrated in Stephen Scalia's garden on Governor Nicholls Street (overleaf) today. The street was named for Francis T. Nicholls, a Civil War hero who was twice governor of Louisiana.

Many French Quarter cottages are entered via a stoop like those on Ursulines Street (above) and Dumaine Street (overleaf). In the days before air conditioning, residents would catch a breeze while chatting with their neighbors on these simple porches. Ursulines Street is named for the old Ursuline Convent (right). Originally built as French military headquarters in 1752, it is the oldest building of record in the Mississippi Valley. Saved by a "bucket brigade" from a fire that destroyed four-fifths of the city in 1788, the building became a convent, then an orphanage. Today it is an archive and museum of New Orleans's Roman Catholic archdiocese.

French Quarter balcony apartments like those on Dumaine Street (left and above) are highly prized. They sit serenely above the commotion, are fun to decorate, and give residents a pleasant perch on which to enjoy coffee or a meal. They are also an ideal perch from which to enjoy Carnival or an impromptu parade. First-time guests on these balconies may be stunned to see ships on the Mississippi River passing at eye level, for the streets of the Quarter lie well below the river. New Orleans's gleaming Central Business District (overleaf), viewed from atop the New Orleans Riverside Hilton and Towers, stands in remarkable contrast to the neighboring old Vieux Carré.

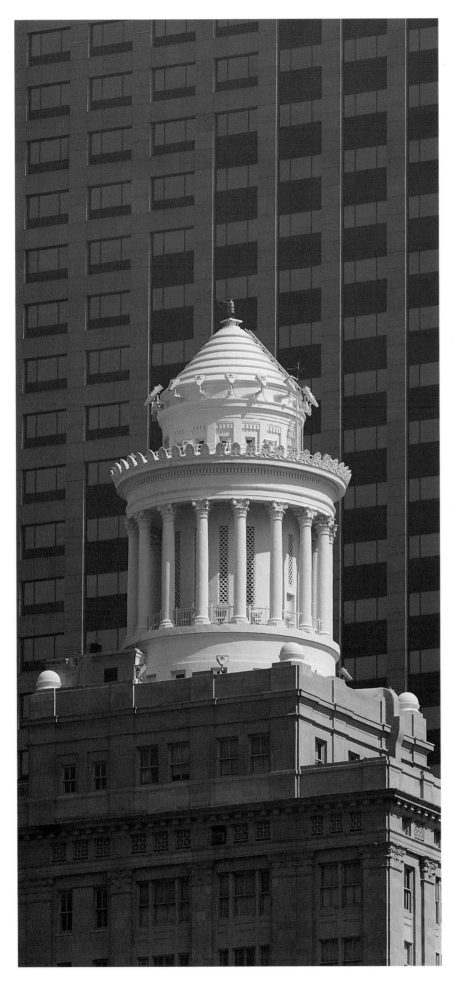

Canal Street (opposite) had fallen on hard times before a vibrant renewal replaced many vacant units and cluttered retail spaces with fine hotels and lively restaurants. The bright-white Hibernia Bank tower (left), which for decades was the most recognizable building on the low-lying New Orleans skyline, is dwarfed by soaring office towers today. In Lafayette Square—the American section's early counterpart to the French Quarter's square—stands a monument to John McDonogh (above), presented to the city by the schoolchildren of New Orleans. McDonogh, a wealthy New Orleans business-man, left his entire fortune to support free schools there and in his native Baltimore.

The sweet sounds of clarinetist Pete Fountain (above) have entertained millions of Dixieland jazz fans on his albums, each Mardi Gras as he leads his "Half-Fast Marching Band" through New Orleans streets, and evenings at his club in the New Orleans Riverside Hilton and Towers. Zesty food and great music come together at the Palace Café on Canal Street. In 1991, as they were converting venerable Oerlein's music store into a lively restaurant and sidewalk café, the owners commissioned artist Marilyn Carter Rougelot to ring the balcony level with a mural featuring New Orleans scenes. In this section (left), piano player "Sweet Emma" and trumpeter Papa Celestin are among the musicians depicted.

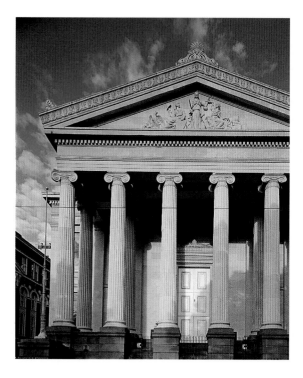

The 1853 Greek Revival Gallier Hall (above) served for more than a century as city hall. Now used for meetings, receptions, weddings, and Carnival events, it is named for noted New Orleans architect James Gallier Jr., who designed it. Perhaps the city's most famous commercial trademark is the Whitney Bank clock, one of which stands on the Whitney Building itself (right) on Common Street downtown. The Whitney and its arch-competitor, Hibernia Bank, were bastions of prudent financial management in a sometimes spendthrift city. The twenty-seven-story, flying-saucer-shaped Louisiana Superdome (overleaf) sports arena and exhibition hall radically changed the profile of the Central Business District.

New Orleans's Warehouse District, along the Mississippi River but away from French Quarter crowds, had deteriorated into a Skid Row of abandoned factories and storehouses. But the Louisiana World Exposition of 1984 centered there—an artistic success but critical and financial disappointment—led to a stunning neighborhood revitalization. The Riverwalk (above), a half-mile-long shopping arcade, connects with the huge convention center on the old fair site. The delightful Restaurant L'Economie (right) was once The Economy, a blue-collar workers' luncheonette. Artists like Luis Colmenares (opposite) have turned many of the district's warehouses into studios and loft apartments. Colmenares is a "metal artist" who turns scraps of iron, tin, and even silver and gold into highly prized furniture and decorative signs.

The 1850 Grinnan Villa (above) stood out in what was once the rowdy Uptown port of Lafayette, an early American suburb of French New Orleans. Its designer, Henry Howard—architect of a score of great Louisiana houses, including the Madewood, Nottaway, and Belle Grove plantation manors—made this house deliberately asymmetrical, starting with a front door that is off center. Howard died poverty-stricken and alone, of paralysis, in New Orleans's Charity Hospital, where he had designed the new syphilitic wards and dissecting rooms. After a restoration at Grinnan Villa in the early 1990s, the dining room (opposite) was returned to its early splendor. An Uptown institution since 1915 has been the Roman Chewing Candy man's roving mule cart (overleaf), now operated by the founder's grandson, Ron Kottemann. He boils, whips, and pulls taffy into long sticks right onboard as the cart rolls through town.

Not all of Uptown New Orleans is an enclave of fashionable mansions. The area has a host of old-timey shops and restaurants, including colorful Casamento's seafood restaurant (above) on Magazine Street. There, waitress Alma Griffin serves television personality and newspaper essayist Ronnie Virgets the house specialty—ice-cold "ersters" on the half shell. Once a racing writer with the nom de plume "Railbird Ronnie," Virgets seeks out the "real New Orleans" for his whimsical "Remoulade" television features. He has often stopped at Fred Hahn and Joan Wright's Uptown Fruit Stand (right), which they set up on South Carrollton Avenue in the city's first "streetcar suburb." Save, perhaps for "Jersey" tomatoes from the state of that name, Creole tomatoes are acclaimed as the sweetest in the land.

Uptown's premier restaurant is Commander's Palace, founded in 1880 by Emile Commander and soon patronized by distinguished neighborhood families. But by the 1920s the site was a notorious brothel. It was rehabilitated and, beginning in the 1970s, turned by Ella, Dottie, Dick, and John Brennan into a culinary legend. Commander's features a jazz brunch in its romantic courtyard (opposite) on Saturdays and Sundays. The restaurant, on Washington Avenue, cannot be easily missed: its main building is painted a shocking turquoise—faithful to its color in bawdier days. A few blocks away on Napoleon Avenue, vampire mystery novelist Anne Rice bought Saint Elizabeth's asylum (left), once an orphanage. Even statelier mansions can be found on Saint Charles Avenue (overleaf), down the street.

Italianate and Greek Revival were architectural styles of choice along Saint Charles Avenue (above). Wealthy sugar and cotton planters had earlier built stupendous homes in the Garden District, and the procession of grand mansions continued up Saint Charles at the turn of the century, especially once the streetcar line—now the nation's oldest still in operation—served the 1884 World's Industrial & Cotton Exposition. Residents now consider the streetcar a "movable museum." Several Saint Charles Avenue mansions were designed by Thomas Sully, whom the National Trust for Historic Preservation calls "the king of Uptown architecture." Sully, who himself lived on the avenue, loved big porches, neoclassical columns, and "living halls" opening to the big downstairs rooms. One of the eclectic Victorian mansions on Saint Charles is the House of Broel (opposite), which includes a delightful doll house museum and frequently hosts receptions, weddings, and teas.

1510 St

Tulane and Loyola universities' Uptown campuses (right) are separated by only a hedge. In the foreground is Tulane's Dinwiddie Hall. Behind it is Loyola's Holy Name of Jesus Church, inspired by England's Canterbury Cathedral. The campus church's lofty spires are among the city's most impressive. Loyola, the South's largest Roman Catholic university, moved from a downtown location in 1911. So did private, nonsectarian Tulane seventeen years earlier. It began as the Medical College of Louisiana and was rechristened to honor benefactor Paul Tulane. Tulane's medical school is also in the Central Business District. The Christ and the Samaritan Fountain at Notre Dame Seminary (opposite), around the riverbend on South Carrollton Avenue, was the centerpiece sculpture at the 1984 Louisiana World Exposition's Vatican Pavilion.

Many cottages at the Riverbend in old Carrollton—once a resort favored for its fresh air and river views—are small but distinctive. Some are delicately ornamented (top right). Others are classic "shotgun houses" (bottom right). These are narrow homes, often built as inexpensive rental property, in which rooms follow one behind the other. The name is pure imagery: the idea is that a shotgun blast through the front door would carry straight out the back door. The Pitot House (opposite), named for owner James Pitot, the first elected mayor of New Orleans, is one of the few remaining West Indies-style houses that lined Bayou Saint John in the 1700s. It is not far from resplendent City Park, whose lagoon (overleaf) lures artists, picnickers, and daydreamers.

Verdant City Park, on the old Allard Plantation grounds, grew to include the Museum of Art, golf courses, tennis courts, a swimming pool, a sports stadium, and whimsical attractions like the "Touch of Saint Patty's" great oak tree (opposite). The display is part of the prison art program run by Orleans Parish sheriff's deputies and staff. The Dixie Brewery in Mid-City (left) was the last local holdout once massive national advertising campaigns and improved distribution by national breweries doomed other local brewers like Regal, Jax, and Falstaff. The world's longest over-water bridge, the twenty-four-mile, dual-span Lake Pontchartrain Causeway (overleaf), ties suburban Metairie to once-rustic North Shore communities like Mandeville and Covington. Their piney woods, cooler temperatures, and comfortable distance from urban problems turned the North Shore into a hot real-estate market.

Suburban Metairie contains lavish homes but also some of the area's most congested shopping areas. Many people visit not the living but the dead at the sprawling Metairie Cemetery (right) where, as S. Frederick Starr pointed out in his revealing book of essays called New Orleans UnMasqued, Confederate heroes and Louisiana luminaries are "at rest above the water table." Metairie's lavish Longue Vue House and Gardens (opposite) is an eight-acre estate once owned by cotton broker Edgar Bloom Stern, who ran Louisiana's first television station, and his wife, Edith, who was the daughter of Sears magnate Julius Rosenwald. Now open for tours and research into architectural and landscape design, Longue Vue features both wild and incomparably cultivated gardens, as well as ponds and outdoor sculptures.

Slidell, near the
Mississippi line, is
reached via the often-
congested Interstate
10 "High Rise" bridge
that soars over the
eastern tip of Lake
Pontchartrain. It's a
working-class com-
munity with a sur-
prising number of
amenities, including
delectable restau-
rants. At Assunta's,
Chef "Mama
Assunta"—Naples,
Italy, native Assunta
Vitegliano Young—
makes pasta and

sinfully rich sauces
from scratch (above).
Parties of four or
more at Slidell's
Chateau Bleu (right)
enjoy dishes like
Veal Marguery and
Rouladens of Beef
Novelle in a private
dining room. And
Chateau Bleu caters!
Closer to town—
but still far from the
French Quarter—the
architecture, rather
than the food, is the
attraction at a ship
captain's "steamboat
house" (overleaf).

New Orleans's "back of town" contains some of the city's most idiosyncratic delights, like a mom-and-pop store (top right) that serves the New Orleans equivalent of a submarine or hoagie sandwich: the "po-boy." Usually this epicurean's nightmare is stuffed with Italian lunch meats, roast beef, fried oysters, or shrimp, slathered with mayonnaise, and topped with dashes of pepper sauce. Many musical celebrities have come out of the poor Ninth Ward, where pop singer Antoine "Fats" Domino maintains a home and studio (bottom right). In another poor neighborhood, Trémé, near Congo Square—where slaves were once encouraged to chant and dance for the amusement of their masters—stands a statue that honors another New Orleans superstar, trumpeter Louis Armstrong (opposite). "Satchmo" broke out of poverty to gain worldwide fame.

Faubourg Marigny, immediately down-river from the French Quarter, was a retreat for ruling Creoles and a place where free persons of color owned as much as 40 percent of the cottages. But it was developed by a slaveholder, Bernard de Marigny, an enthusiastic duelist who taught the deadly practice to neighboring Americans. The Marigny is now home to a community theater and small businesses, including the big Battistella's Seafood wholesaler (left). America's famous "Cajun Chef," Paul Prudhomme (above), whose restaurant and videotapes introduced his family recipes to an enthusiastic worldwide audience, maintains a homespun test kitchen there. Alongside the French Quarter on Rampart Street— once the center of the notorious Storyville red-light district—a number of structures with delicate ironwork (overleaf) remain.

117

Charles Étienne Gayarré was one of the city's first great historians, who wrote (in French) a four-volume history of Louisiana in the early nineteenth century. There is a plaza in his honor on Esplanade Avenue. In it stands a classic figure of Liberty atop a red-sandstone pedestal (above), moved to that location from the 1884 Cotton Centennial fairsite. In several parts of town, simple shotgun houses like one in the Bywater area downriver of the Faubourg Marigny (left), have been expanded by simply tacking on conventional-sized additions in the back. Yet, at first glance, from the street they appear as tiny as other shotgun units.

The Algiers neighborhood lies across the imposing Greater New Orleans Bridge on the "West Bank," which, due to the Mississippi River's serpentine turns, is actually east of the French Quarter in spots. The origin of the name is certain. One explanation ties "Algiers" to early pirate activity as fierce as that on North Africa's Barbary Coast. Mixed among ordinary working-class cottages, historic churches and synagogues, modest stores, and abandoned shops are beautifully landscaped homes like Frank Fasullo's shotgun (right) and Joe and Jessie Scalia's Victorian (above). The latter was once owned by a millwright who salvaged its grand staircase from the 1884 Cotton Centennial fairsite.

New Orleans visits often extend to the area's lush surroundings, including the bayous and swamps of the Atachafalaya Basin in Southwest Louisiana and the mysterious wetlands (opposite) off Lake Maurepas. On Avery Island—which is not an island at all—south of New Iberia, visitors get an unexpected change of pace. They can watch peppers being grown, mashed, cured, and bottled for world-famous Tabasco sauce, and also see an exotic bird sanctuary (above). There, once-threatened egrets nest peacefully. Near Baton Rouge on the Great River Road are several glorious antebellum plantation homes, including Parlange (overleaf) in the town of New Roads. This raised French Colonial home is the largest of its type remaining in the country. Parlange has always been a working farm—indigo at first, then cotton, corn, cattle, and sugarcane. Soybeans are the staple now.

Index

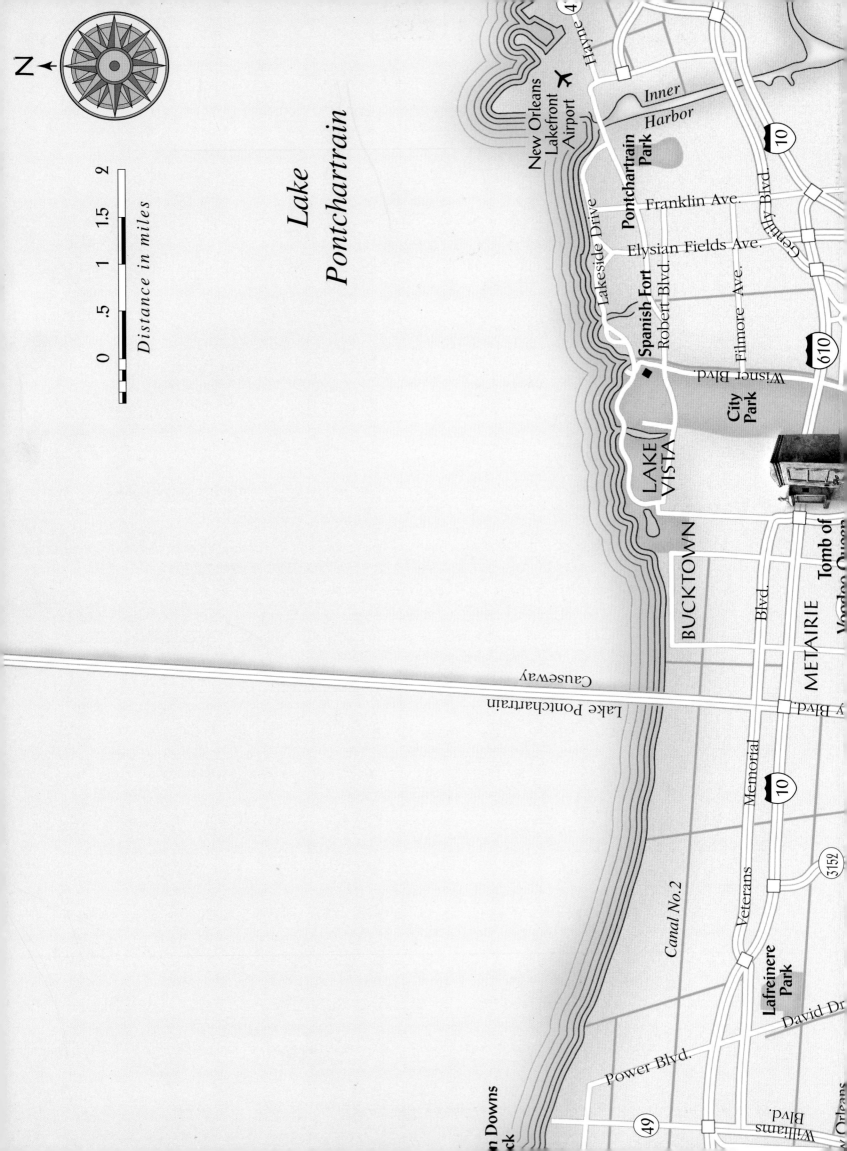

N ←

Distance in miles

0   .5   1   1.5   2

Lake Pontchartrain

Lake Pontchartrain Causeway

New Orleans Lakefront Airport

Inner Harbor

Hayne

4

10

Pontchartrain Park

Franklin Ave.

Century Blvd

Lakeside Drive

Elysian Fields Ave.

Filmore Ave.

Spanish Fort

Robert Blvd.

610

Wisner Blvd.

City Park

LAKE VISTA

BUCKTOWN

Blvd.

METAIRIE

Tomb of Voodoo Queen

Canal No.2

Memorial

Veterans

10

3152

Lafreinere Park

David Dr

Power Blvd.

49

Williams Blvd.

Orleans

n Downs ck